Bubba's Beez
Honey from the Hive
Cookbook

Meredith Duke

DEDICATION

This cookbook is dedicated first and foremost to God, our loving, Heavenly Father. To God goes all the glory and honor.

"Eat honey, my son, for it is good; honey from the comb is sweet to your taste. Know also that wisdom is like honey for you: If you find it, there is a future hope for you, and your hope will not be cut off."

Proverbs 24:13-14

CONTENTS

WELCOME!

Being a beekeeping family has its perks, one of which is being able to not only use "homegrown" honey in our home, but also the beeswax. We get many requests for recipes and thought it would be a wonderful idea to share these recipes, tips and tricks with you in a cookbook.

Inside you will find not only cooking recipes, but how to clean beeswax (although there are a few, I've listed the way that we clean the wax) and ways to use beeswax.

Our hope is that you will not only enjoy Bubba's Beez honey on its own, but that you will also branch out and try new recipes.

Feel free to contact us with questions, suggestions or just to say hi. We'd love to hear from you!

From our home to yours, we pray that God blesses you and keeps you safe. May His face shine up you, be gracious unto you and give you peace.

Blessings,

The Duke Family
www.bubbasbeez.com
bubbasbeez@hotmail.com

1 CONDIMENTS & BEVERAGES

Peach Honey Butter

Honey Butter

Honey Mustard Dressing

Honey Lime Dressing

Cranberry Honey Sauce

Hot Spiced Cider

Honey Limeade

Green Tea & Honey Smoothie

Fresh Fruit Freeze

Orange-Berry Shake

Lessons from the Hive:
Bees are Environmentally Friendly

Bees are remarkable little creatures. Just by observing them we can learn a lot. Do you know that bees are "green" insects? Nothing goes to waste in the hive. Pollen and nectar collected from flowers help to make the honey. The pollen can be safely collected from a hive and used on snacks (like yogurt) or in drinks (like smoothies). Once honey is harvested, the wax can be cleaned and used for many additional products and household uses (beauty treatments, to un-stick drawers, or even used to protect wooden furniture). The excess propolis can also be scraped off the frames and used to make a tincture for scrapes and cuts. And let's not forget the wonderful honey itself which can be used for cooking, baking or in beauty treatments, too.

Peach Honey Butter

2 cups peeled, pitted and ground peaches
1 cup honey

Put peaches and honey in a heavy bottom saucepan. Bring to a boil and then turn down the heat to medium and cook until quite thick (about an hour), stirring frequently.

❂ ❂ ❂

Honey Butter

1 cup butter, softened
1/2 cup honey
1 teaspoon vanilla

Whip butter until light and fluffy. Slowly add the honey and vanilla. Adding the honey too rapidly makes the honey lose its thick, fluffy consistency. Whip 2-3 minutes longer. Cover and refrigerate.

Honey Mustard Dressing

1/4 cup mayonnaise
1 tablespoon prepared mustard
1 tablespoon honey
1/2 tablespoon lemon juice

In a small bowl, whisk all ingredients together. Store covered in the refrigerator.

Honey Lime Dressing

1/2 cup honey
1/2 cup lime juice
1/2 teaspoon cinnamon

Place all ingredients in the blender and blend.

Cranberry and Honey Sauce

3/4 cup fresh cranberries
1 cup water
3 tablespoons sugar
2 tablespoons honey
1 tablespoon lemon juice

In a medium saucepan combine cranberries, 1 cup water and sugar. Bring to boiling, stirring to dissolve sugar. Boil gently, uncovered for 10 minutes, stirring occasionally. Add honey and lemon juice. Return to boiling. Reduce heat; simmer 3 minutes more. Cool slightly. Remove 1/4 cup of the cranberries with a slotted spoon; set aside. Transfer remaining mixture to a blender; cover and blend until almost smooth. Strain to remove skins. Stir reserved berries into strained mixture. Cover; chill 2 hours or until completely chilled. Makes 1 cup.

❁❁❁

Hot Spiced Cider

7 1/2 cups apple cider or apple juice
1/4 cup honey
6 inches stick cinnamon
1 teaspoon whole allspice
1 teaspoon whole cloves
2 strips orange peel

In a large saucepan combine cider and honey. For the spice bag, place cinnamon, allspice, cloves, and the orange peel in the center of a 100% cotton cheesecloth. Bring corners of the cheesecloth together and tie with a clean string. Add spice bag to the saucepan with cider mixture.

Bring mixture to boiling; reduce heat. Simmer, covered, for 15 minutes. Remove spice bag and discard.

Honey Limeade

1 cup lime juice
2/3 cup white sugar
2 tablespoons honey
5 cups water

Make a simple syrup by dissolving the sugar and honey with the lime juice on medium high heat. Once dissolved, pour the syrup into a pitcher and add the water. Chill in the refrigerator.

Green Tea & Honey Smoothie

2 cups frozen unsweetened mixed fruit
3/4 cup brewed green tea
3 tablespoons honey
1 tablespoon lemon juice

In a blender, combine all ingredients; blend until smooth and frothy. Serve immediately.

Fresh Fruit Freeze

1 1/2 cups chilled carbonated water
1 1/2 cups crushed ice
1 cup of your favorite fruit mix (strawberries, blueberries,
mango, peaches, etc.)
1/4 cup honey
1/4 cup freshly squeezed lime juice

In a blender combine all ingredients, cover and blend. Pour
into chilled glasses. Serve immediately.

❈❈❈

Orange-Berry Shake

1 cup boiling water
2 orange-flavored herbal tea bags
1 cup frozen strawberries
1/2 cup Greek yogurt
2 tablespoons honey

In a small saucepan, pour boiling water over tea bags; cover
and brew 5 minutes. Remove tea bags; cool. In blender, process
tea and remaining ingredients until smooth.

2 BREADS

Buttermilk & Honey Pancakes

Honey Waffles

Sweet Honey Cornbread

Honey Muffins

Homemade Biscuits

Baked Oatmeal

Honey Beer Bread

Wheat Bread

Honey Challah

Banana Bread

06/03/2010

Lessons from Bubba:
Bee Natural

It is astounding at the rate the bees are dying off in the U.S., let alone the world. In order to protect the bees, we must each do our part and reduce the amount of pesticides or chemicals we use around our homes or businesses. Even the seeds we purchase for gardens can be tainted with systemic pesticides (they are embedded within the seed itself to keep insects from killing the plant).

Here are a few alternatives to try:
- Apple cider vinegar can be used as a general household cleaner.
- Diatomaceous Earth can be used to kill ants or other insects in the garden and around the home.
- Plant heirloom or open-pollinated seeds in your home garden. They do not contain pesticides within the seed and you can save the seeds for next year's garden.

Buttermilk & Honey Pancakes

1 cup all purpose flour
1/2 cup oatmeal
1 teaspoon baking powder
1/2 teaspoon baking soda
1/4 teaspoon salt
1 large egg, lightly beaten
1 cup buttermilk
2 tablespoons honey

Heat a cast iron skillet on medium heat. Stir first 5 ingredients in a medium bowl. Add egg, buttermilk and honey, stirring until combined. The batter should still be lumpy.

Pour spoon-sized batter onto a hot, lightly greased cast iron skillet. Cook until top is covered with bubbles and edges look cooked. Turn and cook 1-2 more minutes. Repeat with remaining batter.

❂ ❂ ❂

Honey Waffles

2 1/2 cups of flour
1 cup rolled oats
1 tablespoon plus 1 teaspoon baking powder
3/4 teaspoon salt
1 1/2 tablespoons honey
2 large eggs, beaten
2 cups milk
3/4 cup applesauce

Combine first four ingredients in a large bowl. Combine honey, eggs, milk, and applesauce; add to flour mixture, stirring with a wire whisk just until dry ingredients are moistened. Cook in a preheated, oiled waffle iron until golden.

Sweet Honey Cornbread
3/4 cup plus 2 tablespoons cornmeal
6 tablespoons all-purpose flour
1/4 teaspoon baking soda
2 teaspoons baking powder
1/2 teaspoon salt
3/4 cup buttermilk
1/4 cup canola oil
2 tablespoons honey
1 large egg
1 teaspoon butter

Preheat the oven to 450° F. Put the 1 teaspoon butter in a 10" cast iron pan and place in the oven until the butter melts.

Combine first 5 ingredients in a bowl. Stir in buttermilk and next 3 ingredients until well blended. Slowly pour into the preheated pan and bake for 10-12 minutes or until golden brown.

❁❁❁

Honey Muffins
(Laura Ingalls Wilder)
2 tablespoons honey
1 cup milk
1 beaten egg
2 tablespoons melted butter
2 cups graham flour
1/2 teaspoon salt
1 1/2 teaspoons baking powder

Preheat oven to 350° F. Mix the honey, milk, egg and butter together in a bowl. Mix the flour, salt and baking powder in a separate bowl. Add to the liquid mixture.

Bake in greased muffin pans until golden brown.

Homemade Biscuits

You might be wondering why I included a biscuit recipe in this cookbook. It does not contain honey, but these biscuits are truly scrumptious with honey drizzled on them right after they come out of the oven, piping hot and delicious.

2 1/4 cups flour
2 1/4 teaspoons baking powder
1 1/8 teaspoon salt
1 tablespoon sugar
1/2 cup butter
1 large egg, lightly beaten
1/2 cup milk
1 tablespoon butter, melted

Combine flour, baking powder, salt, and sugar in a medium bowl; stir well. Cut in shortening with a pastry blender until mixture is crumbly.

Combine egg and milk; add to flour mixture, stirring just until dry ingredients are moistened. Turn dough out onto a lightly floured surface and knead 3 to 4 times.

Roll dough to ½-inch thickness and cut with a biscuit cutter. Place on an ungreased baking sheet. Bake at 450° F for 10 minutes or until golden. Remove from oven and brush with melted butter.

Drizzle honey over hot biscuits and enjoy.

Baked Oatmeal

(New Harvest Homestead Forum)

This is the only way our children will eat oatmeal. Serve it with honey right out of the oven. It's perfect for those cold winter mornings.

    2 cups quick oats
    1/2 cup brown sugar
    1/2 teaspoon salt
    1 1/2 teaspoons baking powder
    1 teaspoon cinnamon
    1 large egg, beaten
    1/3 cup applesauce
    3/4 cup milk

Preheat oven to 350° F. Mix together dry ingredients. In a separate bowl mix egg, applesauce and milk. Add wet ingredients to the dry ingredients and mix well.

Pour into a greased pie plate. Bake for 20-25 minutes or until done.

Serve with honey.

Honey Beer Bread

3 cups all-purpose flour
1 tablespoon sugar
1 tablespoon baking powder
1 teaspoon salt
1 (12-ounce) beer (your favorite kind)
3 tablespoons honey
4 tablespoons unsalted butter, melted and cooled slightly

Preheat oven to 350°F. Grease a 9x5-inch loaf pan; set aside.

In a large bowl, whisk together flour, sugar, baking powder and salt. Add the beer and honey; stir with a wooden spoon until thoroughly combined.

Spread the batter evenly in the prepared loaf pan and drizzle the melted butter evenly over the top of the batter. Bake until the loaf is golden brown and a thin knife inserted into the center comes out clean, about 50 to 60 minutes. Allow to cool to room temperature before slicing.

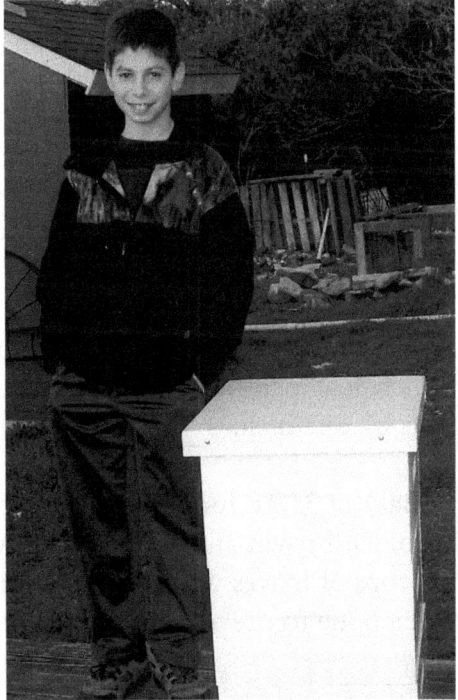

Wheat Bread

This bread is extremely easy to make with a stand mixer.

3 cups warm water (warm to the touch)
2 packages active dry yeast
2/3 cup honey, divided
5 cups unbleached flour
3 tablespoons butter, melted
1 tablespoon salt
3 1/2 cups whole wheat flour
2 tablespoons butter, melted

In a large mixing bowl, using the paddle attachment, mix water, yeast, and 1/3 cup honey. Add 5 cups unbleached flour, and stir to combine. Let set for 30 minutes, or until the mixture is big and bubbly.

Mix in 3 tablespoons melted butter, 1/3 cup honey, and salt. Stir in 2 cups whole wheat flour. To knead, replace the paddle attachment with the dough hook. The dough should start pulling away from the edges of the bowl and make a ball. You may need to use an additional 2 to 4 cups of whole wheat flour. Once the dough is tacky to the touch, place in a greased bowl, turning once to coat the surface of the dough. Cover with a dishtowel. Let rise in a warm place until doubled.

Punch the dough and divide into 3 loaves. Place in greased 9 x 5 inch loaf pans, and allow to rise until dough has topped the pans by one inch.

Bake at 350°F for 25 to 30 minutes. The bread is done when it is golden brown and sounds hollow when tapped. Lightly brush the tops of loaves with 2 tablespoons melted butter or margarine when done to prevent crust from getting hard. Cool completely.

Honey Challah

1 package active dry yeast
1 1/4 cups warm water, divided
5 1/2 cups all-purpose flour
2 teaspoons salt
1/2 cup honey
2 eggs
1/4 cup butter or margarine, melted
1 egg yolk

In small bowl, combine yeast and 1/4 cup warm water. Let stand 10 minutes, until yeast bubbles and doubles in volume (this is called "proofing the yeast").

In large mixing bowl, combine flour and salt; add honey, eggs, and margarine or butter. Add proofed yeast and mix until well combined. Turn dough onto lightly floured work surface; knead until dough is smooth and elastic. Place dough in lightly greased bowl. Cover with a towel and let rise in warm, draft-free place until doubled.

Punch down dough; cover and let rise again until doubled. Punch down dough; form into a ball. Place on lightly greased baking sheet. Mix egg yolk with 1 tablespoon water. Brush over formed Challah. Let rise until almost doubled in size.

Bake at 350°F for 35 to 40 minutes until golden brown and hollow when underside is tapped. Remove from oven and cool before slicing. Makes 1 loaf.

Banana Bread

1/2 cup honey
1/3 cup butter or margarine
1 teaspoon vanilla
2 eggs
1/2 cup all-purpose flour
3/4 cup whole wheat flour
1/2 cup quick-cooking oats
1 teaspoon baking powder
1/2 teaspoon salt
1 teaspoon ground nutmeg
1 cup mashed ripe banana

Cream honey and butter in large bowl with electric mixer until fluffy. Beat in vanilla. Add eggs, one at a time, beating well after each addition.

Combine dry ingredients in small bowl; add to honey mixture alternately with bananas, blending well.

Spoon batter into greased and floured 9x5x3-inch loaf pan. Bake in preheated 325°F oven 50 to 55 minutes or until a wooden toothpick inserted near center comes out clean. Cool in pan on a wire rack 15 minutes. Remove from pan; cool completely on a wire rack.

3 MEAT DISHES

Honey-Glazed Grilled Chicken

Honey Baked Chicken

Maple & Honey Glazed Ham

Honey Grilled Salmon

Hawaiian Steak

Herbed Turkey Breast

Chicken Kabobs

Beef Stew

03/23/2011

Lessons from the Hive:

Don't Be A Sluggard

Did you know that bees will literally fly their wings off? Our road is a half-mile long. We've seen bees walking their way towards their hive with no wings at all – and they're a quarter of a mile away! They work 24 hours a day and 7 days a week. They don't take vacations or sleep. They are constantly working. In the summer bees may only live four to six weeks, but in the winter they can live up to four to six months simply because they are not working as hard or flying far and wide to gather nectar or pollen. The hive tends to slow down in the winter, even the queen does not lay eggs in the winter.

Imagine all that we could accomplish by following this same work ethic. It's not that we should become workaholics and neglect family and friends. Humans were created in the image of God and are entirely different from the bee. However, there is nothing wrong with working hard. Even God worked six days and rested on the seventh.

Honey-Glazed Grilled Chicken

1 whole chicken (4-5 pounds)
1 1/2 tablespoons kosher salt
1 tablespoon baking soda
1 can beer (12 oz.)

Glaze
1 teaspoon cornstarch
1 tablespoon water
1/2 cup honey
1/2 cup peach jam
1/4 cup white wine vinegar
2 tablespoons unsalted butter
2 tablespoons Dijon mustard

Combine salt and baking soda, rub onto chicken. Discard half of the beer. Place half-filled beer can in a beer can roasting rack. Set chicken, cavity side down, on top of beer can. Cover chicken with plastic wrap and refrigerate until ready to grill. Heat charcoal or gas grill to medium-low heat (325° F). Set prepared chicken on indirect-heat side of grill, cover and roast for 1 hour and 15 minutes, rotating once.

While chicken is roasting, combine cornstarch and one tablespoon of water in small cup and set aside. Combine remaining glaze ingredients in saucepan and heat on medium low until glaze begins to bubble; cook for 30 minutes to reduce to ¾ cup. Stir cornstarch mixture again and add to simmering glaze.

Once chicken breast temperature reaches 140°, brush with glaze and continue to roast with grill lid closed for 30 minutes, checking every 15 minutes to make sure glaze doesn't burn. Remove chicken from grill when internal temperature reaches 165°. Place roasted chicken on serving platter and brush liberally with remaining glaze, cover loosely with foil and allow to rest for 20 minutes.

Honey Baked Chicken

1 (2-3 pound) whole chicken cut into pieces
1/4 teaspoon ground black pepper
1 egg yolk
1/2 teaspoon garlic powder
1 1/2 tablespoons honey
2 teaspoons salt
4 tablespoons butter, melted

Preheat the oven to 325°.

Rub the chicken pieces with the garlic powder, salt and pepper. In a small bowl, beat egg yolk with honey and butter, then brush this mixture over chicken pieces. Place chicken pieces, skin side down, in a lightly greased 9x13 inch baking dish.

Bake for 45-60 minutes or until chicken is cooked through and juices run clear, basting with remaining butter. Just before serving, turn chicken over and bake for another 10-15 minutes to cook the skin on the other side.

Maple and Honey Glazed Ham

1 bone-in spiral sliced half ham or butt
1 cup brown sugar
1 cup maple syrup
1 cup honey
1 teaspoon ground allspice
1 teaspoon ground nutmeg
1 teaspoon ground coves
1 teaspoon Dijon mustard

Prepared ham according to package directions.

To make the glaze: Stir together brown sugar, syrup, honey, allspice, nutmeg, cloves and mustard in medium bowl; set aside.

Brush glaze on ham 30 minutes before ham is cooked through. Continue baking ham uncovered. Carve and serve.

Honey Grilled Salmon

1 teaspoon ground ginger
1 teaspoon garlic powder
1/3 cup soy sauce
1/3 cup orange juice
1/4 cup honey
1 green onion, chopped
1 1/2-pound salmon fillet

In a large self-closing plastic bag, combine ginger, garlic, soy sauce, orange juice, honey, and green onion; mix well. Place salmon in bag and seal tightly. Turn bag gently to distribute marinade. Refrigerate for 15 to 30 minutes.

Preheat an outdoor grill for medium heat and lightly oil grate.

Remove salmon from marinade, shake off excess, and discard remaining marinade. Grill for 12 to 15 minutes per inch of thickness, or until the fish flakes easily with a fork.

Hawaiian Steak

1/3 cup pineapple juice
3 tablespoons honey
1 tablespoon soy sauce
2 tablespoons chopped green onions
1 teaspoon garlic powder
1 pound boneless loin steaks or flank steak
2 teaspoons cornstarch

Combine the pineapple juice, honey, soy sauce, onions and garlic powder in a shallow, non-metallic dish. Add the steak; turn to coat.

Cover and marinate 15 minutes in refrigerator.

Grill or broil steak 10 minutes on each side (for medium). Stir 2 teaspoons cornstarch into marinade. Pour marinade into a small saucepan; heat until hot and slightly thick. Serve with steak.

Herbed Turkey Breast

1/2 cup honey
1/4 cup orange juice
2 tablespoons butter or margarine, melted
1 1/2 teaspoons sage, dried
1 teaspoon thyme, dried
1 clove garlic, minced
3/4 teaspoon salt
1/4 teaspoon pepper
1 boneless, skinless turkey breast, about 2 lbs.

Preheat oven to 350° F.

Combine honey, orange juice, butter, sage, thyme, garlic, salt and pepper. Place turkey breast on rack set in broiler pan. Brush with some of honey mixture.

Bake, brushing frequently with remaining mixture, turning turkey once, until no longer pink inside. Let stand 5 minutes before slicing.

Chicken Kabobs

1/4 cup vegetable oil
1/3 cup honey
1/3 cup soy sauce
1/4 teaspoon ground black pepper
8 skinless, boneless chicken breast halves, cut into 1-inch cubes
2 cloves garlic
5 small onions, cut into 2 inch pieces
2 red bell peppers, cut into 2 inch pieces
Wooden skewers

In a large bowl, whisk together oil, honey, soy sauce, and pepper. Before adding chicken, reserve a small amount of marinade to brush onto kabobs while cooking. Place the chicken, garlic, onions and peppers in the bowl, and marinate in the refrigerator at least 2 hours (or overnight, if possible).

Preheat the grill for high heat. Soak the wooden skewers in water for at least 30 minutes (to prevent them from burning when on the grill).

Drain marinade from the chicken and vegetables, and discard marinade. Thread chicken and vegetables alternately onto the skewers.

Lightly oil the grill grate. Place the skewers on the grill. Cook for 12 to 15 minutes, until chicken juices run clear. Turn and brush with reserved marinade frequently.

Beef Stew

1/4 cup oil
1 cup flour
2 teaspoons salt
2 teaspoons pepper
1 boneless beef chuck roast (4 pounds), trimmed
1 can (14-1/2 ounces) beef broth
1 cup of your favorite beer
1/2 cup honey
3 garlic cloves, minced
1 teaspoon dried marjoram
1 teaspoon dried thyme
1/4 teaspoon cinnamon
8 small red potatoes
4 medium carrots, cut into 1-inch pieces
2 medium onions, quartered
Salt and pepper to taste

In a large dutch oven, heat the oil on medium-high heat.

Combine the flour, salt and pepper in a small bowl. Rinse the meat and pat dry with paper towels. Lightly cover the roast with flour. When the oil is shimmering and dancing with the heat, brown the roast on all sides.

In a small bowl, combine the broth, beer, honey, garlic, marjoram, thyme, salt, pepper and cinnamon; pour over top of browned meat. Bring it to a boil, reduce heat, cover and let is simmer for 4 hours. Flip the roast two hours later.

Thirty minutes before the roast is finished add the potatoes, onions and carrots. Return to boiling, reduce heat to medium, cover and let it simmer for another 30 minutes. When vegetables are done, slice the meat and serve with warm bread.

4 SIDES & VEGGIES

Honey Glazed Carrots

Steamed Vegetables

Honeyed Sweet Potatoes

Honey-Baked Tomatoes

Honey Applesauce

Fruit Salad with Honey-Wine Syrup

Honey-Orange-Glazed Acorn Squash

Sweet Cornbread Dressing

Honeyed Veggies

Strawberry & Avocado Salad

Lessons from Bubba:
Attracting Bees

If you are interested in attracting bees to your property, here are a few plants that bees love:

-   Texas sage
-   Mexican heather
-   English lavender
-   Flowering rosemary
-   Garden favorites like zucchini, pumpkins, cucumbers and herbs (mint, thyme)
-   Asters
-   Sunflowers
-   Salvia
-   Bee balm
-   Hyssop
-   Bachelor buttons
-   Poppy

Honey Glazed Carrots

1 pound carrots, peeled & sliced
1/4 cup honey

Place sliced carrots in a pot with enough water to cover the carrots. Simmer the carrots until they are soft. Drain the water from the pot. Add the honey to the pot with the carrots and stir until the honey covers all the carrots.

❖❖❖

Steamed Veggies

2 1/4 cups acorn squash, peeled, seeded and cut into chunks
1 turnip, pared and cut into chunks
1 cup carrots, julienned
1 small onion, halved and quartered
1/4 cup honey
2 tablespoons butter, melted
1 teaspoon grated orange peel
1/4 teaspoon ground nutmeg

Steam squash, turnip, carrot and onion over water in covered skillet about 5 minutes or until tender. Drain.

Combine honey, butter, orange peel and nutmeg. Drizzle over vegetables and toss; serve.

Honeyed Sweet Potatoes

2/3 cup honey
1 teaspoon salt
1/2 cup butter, softened
8 sweet potatoes, sliced

Preheat the oven to 350° F. Grease a 9x13 inch baking dish.

In a large bowl, stir together the honey, butter and salt. Add the sweet potatoes and stir to coat. Transfer to the prepared baking dish. Pour any liquid from the bowl over the potatoes.

Cover and bake for 30 minutes in the pre-heated oven, basting frequently.

❁❁❁

Honey-Baked Tomatoes

8 medium-size ripe tomatoes, cut into 1-inch slices
4 teaspoons honey
1/3 cup bread crumbs
1 tablespoon dried tarragon
1 1/2 teaspoons salt
2 teaspoons freshly ground pepper
4 teaspoons butter

Place tomato slices in a single layer in a lightly greased jellyroll pan. Drizzle with honey, spreading honey in recesses.

Stir together bread crumbs, tarragon, salt and pepper; sprinkle evenly over tomato slices. Dot with butter.

Bake at 350° F for 30 minutes or until tomato skins begin to wrinkle. Broil 5 inches from heat 5 minutes or until tops are golden.

Honey Applesauce
3 apples, peeled, cored and diced
1/4 cup honey
1/4 cup apple juice, orange juice or pineapple juice

Place all ingredients in blender or food processor. Puree to desired smoothness.

❀❀❀

Fruit Salad with Honey-Wine Syrup
1/4 cup dry white wine
1/4 cup orange juice
1 tablespoon honey
2 large, ripe cantaloupes (halved, seeded and cut into 1-inch cubes or balls)
1/4 cup chopped fresh mint leaves
1 pint strawberries

Stir together the wine, orange juice and honey in a large bowl until blended. Add the cantaloupe and mint. Toss gently to mix thoroughly. Refrigerate, covered, for at least 4 hours or overnight, stirring occasionally.

Just before serving, hull the strawberries and quarter them. Add the strawberries to the cantaloupe mixture. Toss gently to mix thoroughly. Serve cold.

Honey-Orange-Glazed Acorn Squash

1/2 cup butter, softened
2 tablespoons brown sugar
2 tablespoons honey
4 medium acorn squash
2 teaspoons grated fresh orange rind
1/4 cup fresh orange juice

Stir together butter, brown sugar and honey until smooth.

Cut squash in half. Scoop out seeds and membrane. Arrange squash, cut sides up, on a roasting pan. Spread half of butter mixture evenly on cut sides of squash.

Bake squash, uncovered, at 400° F for 30 minutes.

Stir together remaining butter mixture, grated orange rind, and orange juice in a small saucepan. Cook over low heat until butter melts, and brush half of orange-butter mixture evenly on squash.

Bake, uncovered, 20 more minutes or until squash is tender and golden, basting occasionally with remaining orange-butter mixture.

Transfer to a serving platter and drizzle with any remaining orange-butter mixture.

Sweet Cornbread Dressing

4 cups day-old Sweet Honey Cornbread (recipe on page 12)
1 Italian sausage (4 ounces)
1 cup chopped green bell pepper
1/2 cup minced onion
1/2 cup chopped celery
1 tablespoon minced parsley
1 teaspoon dried thyme leaves, crushed
1 teaspoon salt
1/4 teaspoon ground black pepper
1/3 cup chicken broth
2 tablespoons honey

Place crumbled cornbread in a large bowl.

Remove sausage from casing. In medium skillet, crumble and sauté sausage until brown. Using slotted spoon, remove sausage from skillet and add to cornbread.

Drain all but 1 tablespoon of fat. Return skillet to medium-high heat; stir in bell pepper, onion and celery. Sauté until vegetables are soft, about 5 minutes. Stir in parsley, thyme, salt and pepper. Cool slightly, then add to cornbread.

In small bowl, combine broth and honey. Pour over dressing. Place dressing in a greased 9x9-inch baking dish. Cover dish with foil and bake at 350°F for 20 minutes. Remove foil and bake another 10 minutes until dressing is lightly browned.

Honeyed Veggies

12 small red potatoes, halved
1/4 cup honey
3 tablespoons dry white wine
1 clove garlic, minced
1 teaspoon dried thyme leaves, crushed
1/2 teaspoon salt
1/2 teaspoon pepper
2 zucchini, halved lengthwise and halved again
1 medium eggplant, cut into 1/2-inch thick slices
1 green bell pepper, cut in eighths
1 red bell pepper, cut in eighths
1 large onion, cut in 1/2-inch thick slices

Cover potatoes with water in large saucepan. Bring to a boil and simmer 5 minutes; drain.

Combine honey, wine, garlic, thyme, salt and pepper in small bowl; mix well.

Place potatoes and remaining vegetables on oiled barbecue grill over hot coals. Grill 20 to 25 minutes, turning and brushing with honey mixture every 7 to 8 minutes.

Conventional Oven Directions: Toss vegetables with honey mixture. Bake, uncovered, at 400° F 25 minutes or until tender, stirring every 8 to 10 minutes to prevent burning.

Strawberry & Avocado Salad

   4 tablespoons olive oil
   2 tablespoons honey
   2 tablespoons cider vinegar
   2 teaspoons lemon juice
   4 cups torn salad greens
   2 avocados, peeled, pitted and sliced
   20 strawberries, sliced
   1 cup chopped pecans

In a small bowl, whisk together the olive oil, honey, vinegar, and lemon juice. Set aside.

Place the salad greens in a pretty bowl, and top with sliced avocado and strawberries. Drizzle dressing over everything, then sprinkle with pecans. Refrigerate for up to 2 hours before serving, or serve immediately.

5 DESSERTS & SNACKS

Grapefruit & Orange Salad

Frozen Honeyed Walnuts & Raisins

Fruit Honey Pops

Sweet Spiced Popcorn

Honey Granola Bars

Pear-Goat Cheese Tarts

Chewy Pecan Cookies

Chocolate Honey Rolls

Easy Pecan Sticky Buns

Honey & Banana S'mores

Bubba's Beez Baklava

Lessons from the Hive: Working Together

Bees work together in a close environment, surrounded by each other pretty much all the time (except those that forage for pollen and nectar). They each perform a particular task and in doing so the hive benefits from this cohesion and grows. Bees hold various positions within the hive based on their age beginning with housekeeping (cleaning out cells), undertaking (removing dead bees from the hive), nursing the developing bee larvae, attending to the queen, fanning the hive, making beeswax, protecting the hive and foraging for nectar and pollen.

It amazes me how bees work their way up through the ranks of the hive beginning with the small task of cleaning out their own cell from which they emerged and then progressing to the final position of a field bee, searching for nectar and pollen to bring back to the hive. As each bee does its assigned duty, the hive itself grows and prospers.

Grapefruit & Orange Salad
2 grapefruits
2 oranges
2 tablespoons honey
1 teaspoon cinnamon

Cut the ends off a seedless orange just far enough to expose the flesh. Place orange cut end down and cut away the peel and pith by following the orange's shape. Using a sharp knife cut along the inside of the membranes that separate the orange segments. Slice only down to the center of the orange. Continue around entire orange cutting out each section, leaving the membrane. You should have nicely sliced orange segments without any of the membrane attached.

Slice the segments and place in a bowl.

In a separate small bowl combine the honey and cinnamon. Drizzle over the grapefruit and orange slices and gently combine.

❁❁❁

Frozen Honeyed Walnuts & Raisins
1/4 cup walnuts
1/8 cup raisins
2 teaspoons honey

Combine honey and raisins in a small bowl. Drizzle with honey. Cover the bowl and place it in the freezer. The snack is ready to eat in a few hours.

Fruity Honey Pops

1 cup fruit (strawberries, blueberries, peaches, etc.)
1 cup Greek yogurt
2 tablespoons honey

In a small blender, puree the fruit for 30 seconds. In a small bowl, stir together the yogurt and honey. Fold in the fruit puree. Taste and add more honey or fruit puree as desired. Pour mixture into popsicle molds or small cups, filling about ¾ of the way. Add wooden sticks and freeze for several hours.

❈ ❈ ❈

Sweet Spiced Popcorn

8 cups plain popped popcorn
3/4 cup dry-roasted peanuts
1/4 cup honey
1/4 cup butter
1/2 teaspoon curry powder

Preheat oven to 300°. In large roasting pan combine popcorn and peanuts. In a small saucepan heat and stir honey, butter and curry powder until butter melts. Pour butter mixture over popcorn mixture; gently toss to coat.

Bake for 30 minutes, stirring every 10 minutes. Transfer mixture to a large piece of foil to cool. Store in a tightly covered container at room temperature up to 1 week.

Honey Granola Bars

2 cups rolled oats, uncooked
1 cup all-purpose flour
3/4 cup packed light brown sugar
1/2 cup toasted wheat germ
3/4 teaspoon ground cinnamon
3/4 teaspoon salt
1/2 cup vegetable oil
1/2 cup honey
1 large egg
2 teaspoons vanilla extract

Preheat oven to 350°F. Grease 13"x9" baking pan.

In a large bowl, with wooden spoon, combine oats, flour, brown sugar, wheat germ, cinnamon, and salt until blended. Stir in oil, honey, egg, and vanilla until well combined. Pat oat mixture into prepared pan.

Bake until lightly golden, approximately 30-35 minutes. Cool completely in pan.

When cool, cut into 16 equal size bars.

Pear-Goat Cheese Tarts

1 package refrigerator pie crusts
2 (4 oz.) packages goat cheese, crumbled
1 or 2 ripe pears, chopped
2 tablespoons honey
1/4 teaspoon dried thyme

Unfold piecrusts and cut each in half; cut each half into 3 pieces. Place 1 piece into a lightly greased muffin cup in a muffin pan. Fold and press pastry piece to form a cup shape. Repeat procedure with remaining pieces.

Bake at 375° F for 8 minutes or until edges of pastries are lightly browned. Remove pan to a wire rack.

Stir together goat cheese and next three ingredients. Spoon evenly into pastry shells.

Bake at 375° F for 8 to 10 minutes or until thoroughly heated. Remove to a wire rack and let cool 2 minutes.

Chewy Pecan Cookies

2 cups unbleached flour
1 teaspoon salt
1/2 teaspoon baking powder
1/2 teaspoon baking soda
1/2 cup butter or margarine
1 cup honey
1/2 cup sour cream
2 teaspoons vanilla
2 cups seedless raisins
1 cup quick-cooking rolled oats
1 cup pecans, chopped

In small bowl, combine flour, salt, baking powder and baking soda; set aside.

In large mixing bowl, cream butter; beat in honey in fine stream until well blended. Stir in sour cream and vanilla. Blend in flour mixture and remaining ingredients.

Cover and refrigerate dough about 30 minutes. Drop by rounded spoonful onto well greased cookie sheet.

Bake at 325°F above center of oven 20 to 25 minutes or until lightly browned. Let stand 1 minute, then remove to wire racks to cool.

Chocolate Honey Rolls

(National Honey Board)

 1 cup all purpose flour
 1 teaspoon baking powder
 1 tablespoon coconut oil
 1/2 cup milk
 1 teaspoon vanilla extract
 1 1/2 tablespoons honey
 1 teaspoon cocoa powder

Preheat your oven to 400°F.

In a bowl combine flour, baking powder, coconut oil, milk and vanilla. Mix ingredients until a dough forms. Wrap the dough in plastic wrap and put the dough in the freezer for about 20 minutes to harden slightly.

Once the dough has firmed up, place it between 2 pieces of parchment paper and roll out into a rectangle shape. Drizzle half of the honey over the dough. Sprinkle cocoa powder over the honey. Roll dough into a log shape. Slice the roll into 6 pieces. Place each piece (swirl side up) into a muffin cup.

Bake for about 10 to 12 minutes or until golden. Drizzle remaining honey on top. Serve warm or cool.

Easy Pecan Sticky Buns

2 tablespoons butter or margarine, softened
1 loaf frozen bread dough, thawed
1/3 cup honey
1 teaspoon cinnamon
1 cup finely chopped pecans

Grease 12 muffin cups with butter. Roll out thawed dough on lightly floured board to 12 x 8-inch rectangle.

Mix honey and cinnamon. Using back of spoon, spread in even layer over dough. Sprinkle with pecans.

Roll up dough, starting from long edge and end with seam on bottom. Cut dough roll using clean dental floss into 12 equal-size buns. Place buns, spiral side up, in muffin cups. Cover with a piece of plastic wrap and let rise 30 to 60 minutes or until buns puff and fill cups.

Bake at 350°F for 15 to 20 minutes or until golden. Remove from oven and carefully turn pan upside down onto board, letting syrup drip onto buns before removing them from pan.

NOTE: To use dental floss, slide the floss under the rolled dough. Bring up the ends on either side of the dough, cross and pull down. You'll get a nice clean cut without squishy buns.

Honey & Banana S'mores

12 cinnamon graham crackers, 2x2-inch squares
2 tablespoons smooth peanut butter
2 tablespoons honey
1 medium ripe banana, sliced

Arrange six graham crackers on serving plate. Stir together peanut butter and honey until blended. Spread peanut butter mixture generously over six crackers. Arrange banana slices over peanut butter. Place second graham cracker on top of each.

Bubba's Beez Baklava

Justin Andrews contributed this recipe to our cookbook. He and his wife, Darla Andrews, are the proprietors of Woman To Blame Tie Dyes (www.womantoblametiedyes.com) and have been our Georgetown Market Days booth neighbors for quite some time.

1 (16 oz) package of phyllo dough
1 pound chopped pecans or slivered almonds
1 cup butter
1 teaspoon ground cinnamon
1 cup water
1 1/4 cup Bubba's Beez honey
1 teaspoon vanilla extract

Preheat oven to 350 degrees. Butter the bottoms and sides of a 9" x 13" pan.

Chop nuts and toss with cinnamon. Set aside. Unroll phyllo dough. Cut whole stack to fit pan. Cover phyllo dough with a dampened cloth to keep from drying as you work. Place two sheets of dough in pan, butter thoroughly. Repeat until you have 8 sheets layered. Sprinkle 2-3 tablespoons of nut mixture on top. Top with two sheets of dough, butter, nuts, layering as you go. The top layer should be about 6-8 sheets deep.

Using a sharp knife, cut into diamond or square shapes 3/4 of the way down to the bottom of the pan. Bake for 50 minutes until baklava is golden and crisp.

Make sauce while baklava is baking. Boil honey and water until melted. Add vanilla and simmer 20 minutes.

Remove baklava from oven and immediately spoon sauce over it. Let cool. Finish cutting all the way to the bottom of pan. Serve in cupcake papers.

6 USES FOR BEESWAX

How to Clean Beeswax

Non-Toxic Wood Finish

Ironing Wax

For Thread

Threadlock

Seal Envelopes

Homemade Crayons

More Uses for Hand Balm

Lessons from Bubba: Taking Care of Bees

In the hot summer months bees are constantly looking for water, including pools, fountains or even hummingbird feeders. To keep them out of unwanted areas, try placing another water source nearby (like a bird bath or a bowl of water) and see if that helps. Just remember to add rocks or something in the water so that the bees have something to land on to keep them from drowning.

How to Clean Beeswax

Before you can use beeswax, it first must be cleaned since no one wants to buy lip balm with a bee part in it. At least I wouldn't want to so that makes me assume that others wouldn't want to either.

Before we begin, here are a few key tips to remember:
- Use a pot or utensils that you don't need any longer. Beeswax is very difficult to remove and it's just easier to part with a pot you no longer want or need than to use one of your good ones.
- Do not leave the beeswax unattended. It can easily catch on fire (as any wax can).
- Melt the wax on a lower setting, not high.
- Be patient with this process. It takes awhile.

Now to begin:

- Fill your pot with water to about halfway and add the unclean comb. Don't stuff the pot.
- Turn the heat to medium or medium-low and let it melt. When the beeswax has melted and is boiling with the water, turn off the heat. Remove the pot from the heat and let it cool down completely. This takes some time, so don't hover over it. I'll even allow mine to cool overnight. As the beeswax cools, it'll separate from the water and the dirty particles that were in the comb. The beeswax floats on the top and the other particles and water settle underneath it.
- After it's completely cool, the beeswax will have pulled away from the sides of the pot, making it easy to remove.
- Once you've removed the melted wax, set it on paper towels to drain. On the bottom of the wax there will still be lots of particles, etc. Cut these away with a sharp knife so that all you're left with is a slab of wax. It'll still be somewhat dirty, but that's okay for now.
- Throw out the dirty water (but not down the sink as any particles and beeswax will clog your drain).
- Repeat this process two times to remove the debris.
- When you've removed all the major particles you can, the final step involves melting the wax without the water. Clean the pot as best you can to remove any of the dirty particles and wax. To be safe, you'll want to do this in a double-broiler or at least put your smaller pot in a larger pot of water so that your pot with the

wax does not sit directly on the burner. If the wax gets too hot it can ignite. Add your clean wax to the pot, turn the burner on low.

- While the wax is melting, cut up an old, but clean, pair of stockings. I simply cut the feet off of them and stretch them over the openings of clean, plastic containers (i.e. smaller margarine tubs, yogurt cups, or even milk containers – not the plastic kind).
- Once the wax is completely melted, pour it over the stockings which filter out the final bee particles and dirt so that you end up with clean wax.
- Allow the wax to cool completely (depending on the size of the container and how deep the wax is, this could take several hours).
- Once it's completely cool, you can cut away the container and store your beeswax until you're ready to use it!

❀❀❀

Non-Toxic Wood Finish

Mix equal parts beeswax and mineral oil. Heat in a double boiler until melted. Pour into a container and let it cool. Rub onto toys or wood furniture as a polish or protectant. Buff off the excess.

❀❀❀

Ironing Wax

To clean an iron, rub beeswax over a hot iron. Wipe it off while the iron is still hot.

For Thread

Run your sewing thread against a block of beeswax a few times – it will slide through the fabric easier and prevent longer threads from tangling.

❖❖❖

Threadlock

Use on screws to help prevent them from backing out.

❖❖❖

Unstick a Drawer

Rub beeswax along the rails of the drawer to unstick a drawer.

❖❖❖

Seal Envelopes

Melt wax with a candle and seal with a wax sealer.

❖❖❖

Homemade Crayons

Equal parts grated soap and beeswax

Lightly spray soap molds with vegetable spray. Melt the beeswax in a small can placed in boiling water. Add the grated soap and stir until the soap melts and the mixture is smooth.

Add your choice of food color paste to dye the wax. Pour into the prepared molds and let it cool. When cool, remove the crayons from the molds and test. If you desire a deeper color, re-melt the wax and add more food coloring.

More Uses for Hand Balm
(See recipe on page 62)

- Leather Polish – We rub it into our leather couch and buff off any excess. It leaves our couch supple and protects the leather.
- Food-Grade Wood Protectant – Rub into wooden spoons, cutting boards or countertops. Let it soak in overnight and buff the next day.
- Place a dab on your shoes and rub with an old cloth to add a quick shine.

7 BEAUTY RECIPES

Lip Balm

Hand Balm

Homemade Deodorant

Massage Bar

Solid Perfume

Honey Exfoliating Mask

Honey Hair Rinse

Honey Mask II

Lemon Drop Body Wash

Easy Moisturizer

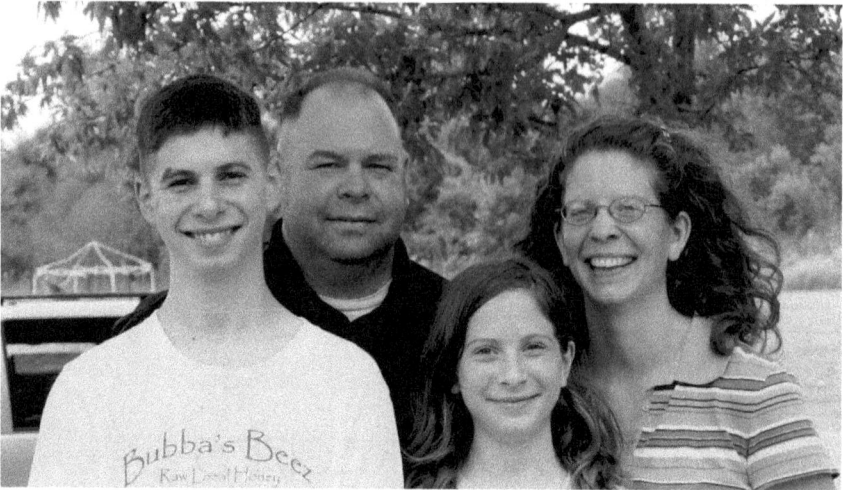

(photo courtesy of John Speasmaker, YourLocalColor.com)

Lessons from the Hive:

Cleanliness is Key

Bees are extremely clean and organized. You will rarely find debris in a hive. Dead bees are thrown outside. Other critters that may find a way in and die will be encased in beeswax to keep them from decaying in the hive.

Take a cue from the bees and try for organization in your own home and life. Clean up the messes and stay on task. You'll be amazed at what you'll accomplish.

Lip Balm

1 cup grapeseed oil
1/2 cup beeswax
2 tablespoons honey

Fill a pot with water halfway. Place grapeseed oil, beeswax and honey in a small glass bowl and place this bowl inside the pot with water (to act as a double boiler). Turn the burner to medium-low and wait for the beeswax to melt. Stir occasionally.

In the meantime, prepare the lip balm tubes. When the beeswax is melted completely pour the mixture into the lip balm tubes or other small containers.

When the lip balms have cooled completely, cap, label and seal.

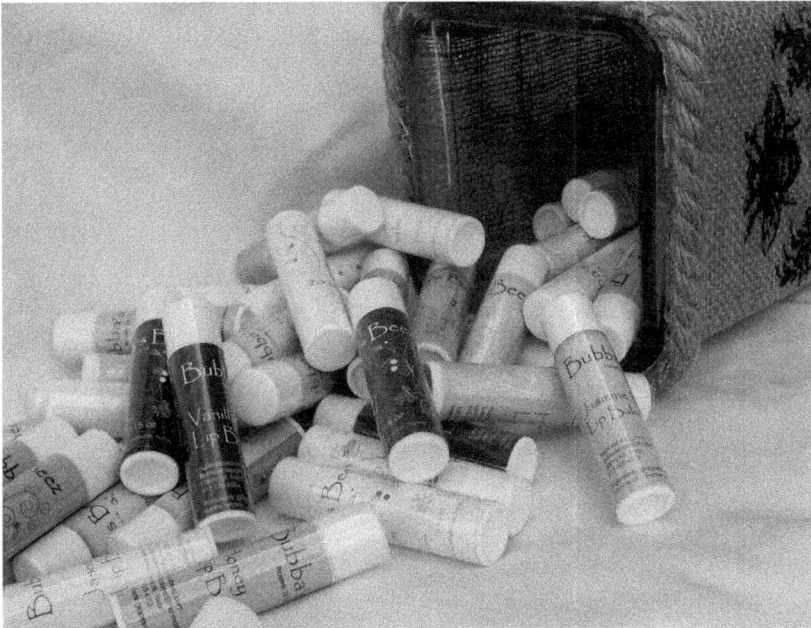

Hand Balm

1/4 cup beeswax
1 cup grapeseed oil

Melt beeswax at low temperature. Add 1 cup oil. Stir. Pour into jar to cool.

Here are a few ideas on how to use this product:
- For softer skin:
  - Apply to your feet after a bath and cover with cotton socks.
  - Rub a bit on your knees and elbows
  - Rub into the cuticles on your fingers
- Apply around your hairline to prevent hair color from bleeding onto your neck, ears and face.
- As a makeup remover
- Mix with epsom salt, sea salt or sugar plus your favorite scent to create a bath scrub.
- As a lip balm
- Apply to cotton swab and place a little in your nasal passage to keep moist.
- Use it for diaper rash or hemorrhoids.

Homemade Deodorant

   1 part baking soda
   1 part hand balm
   1 part talc powder (or cornstarch)
   Essential oil of your choice

Combine baking soda, hand balm and talc in a glass container over a double-boiler. Melt over low heat until it's completely smooth and well-mixed. Add the essential oil. Pour into container (such as an old and empty deodorant container). Cool to room temperature and use as needed.

Note: You can also replace the hand balm with coconut oil.

❀❀❀

Massage Bar

   1 part cocoa butter
   1 part beeswax
   1 part grapeseed oil
   Essential oil(s) of your choice

Melt equal parts of cocoa butter, beeswax and grapeseed oil in a double-boiler. Remove from heat when melted and add the essential oil. Pour into molds and let cool.

These bars melt at body temperature which makes them great for massages or moisturizing.

Solid Perfume
3 parts Jojoba oil
2 parts beeswax
1 part scent

Melt jojoba oil and beeswax over a double boiler until well mixed and integrated. Add the scent. Pour into containers and let cool.

❀❀❀

Honey Exfoliating Mask
1 tablespoon honey
1 tablespoon cornmeal

In a small bowl mix honey and cornmeal. Mix until thoroughly combined. Apply the exfoliating facial mask with gentle, circular motions onto your T-zone, with special attention to the nose, chin and forehead. Leave on for 10 minutes. Rinse with warm water.

❀❀❀

Honey Hair Rinse
4 tablespoons honey
10 tablespoons white vinegar
2 cups water

In a large bowl, add honey, white vinegar and water. Mix until thoroughly combined. Apply this solution as a last step to usual hair regimen when showering. Leave on for 5 minutes and rinse out with warm water to achieve vitalized and radiant hair. Dry and style hair as usual.

Honey Mask II

    1 tablespoon honey
    1/4 banana
    1 teaspoon oatmeal
    1 teaspoon plain yogurt

In a small bowl mash banana and mix in honey, yogurt and oatmeal. Mix until thoroughly combined. Apply onto clean face, avoiding the skin around the eyes. Leave on for 15-20 minutes. Rinse with warm water.

❈❈❈

Lemon Drop Body Wash

(National Honey Board)

    2 cups unscented castile soap
    2 cups honey
    1/2 cup lemon juice
    3-4 drops lemon essential oil, optional

Combine all the ingredients into a bottle and shake.

To use: With sponge or wash cloth, massage desired amount over entire body and rinse. Store in shower; use daily.

❈❈❈

Easy Moisturizer

    Olive Oil
    Honey

Mix equal parts olive oil and honey to create a thick lotion. Rub on dry skin and let sit for 10-20 minutes before rinsing the area for smooth (and staying) results.

8 TIPS FOR COOKING WITH HONEY

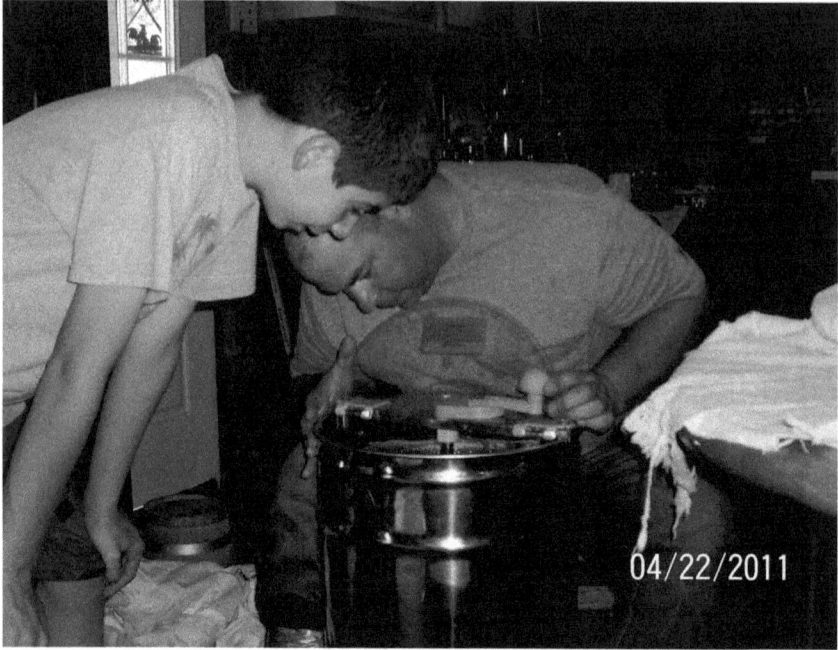

04/22/2011

Lessons from Bubba:
Bee Friendly

Yes, some people are allergic to bees. Yes, they can sting and yes, the stings can hurt (just a little bit). However, if a bee is flying around you, try not to swat it as this can agitate the bee and actually cause it to sting you. Most likely it is only looking for pollen and will soon leave. Be still. Remain calm and you'll have less chance of being stung.

Honey is a wonderful sweetener and can replace sugar in many recipes. Here are a few tips we've learned through the years:

- Store honey at room temperature.
- Substitute up to 1/2 of the sugar in a recipe with honey.
- To get all the honey out of a measuring spoon or cup, lightly coat the spoon or cup with vegetable spray. It slides right out.
- Honey burns quicker and easier than sugar, so if you are using a honey glaze on grilled or baked dishes, add it towards the end of the baking time.

To substitute honey when baking:

- Reduce the liquid in the recipe by 1/4 cup for each cup of honey used.
- Add about 1/2 teaspoon baking soda for each cup of honey used.
- Reduce oven temperature by 25 degrees to prevent over-browning.

The benefits of baking or cooking with honey:

- It is sweeter than sugar so you can use less of it in a recipe and still retain the same level of sweetness.
- It absorbs moisture which allows baked items to stay fresher longer.

How to liquefy crystallized honey:

- Remove the lid from the jar of honey.
- Heat a pot of water on the stove until almost boiling.
- Remove the pot from the stove.
- Place the uncapped jar of honey in the pot.
- Leave it alone until the honey has liquefied and cooled.
- Recap the bottle and enjoy!

Honey is sold by weight, not by volume and is much heavier than water. Here is a conversion chart to help with measurements in the kitchen:

Cups	Ounces	Tablespoons
1/4 cup	3 oz.	4 tablespoons
1/3 cup	4 oz.	5.3 tablespoons
1/2 cup	6 oz.	8 tablespoons
2/3 cup	8 oz.	10.7 tablespoons
3/4 cup	9 oz.	12 tablespoons
1 cup	12 oz.	16 tablespoons

www.ingramcontent.com/pod-product-compliance
Lightning Source LLC
Chambersburg PA
CBHW060419050426
42449CB00009B/2030